FIFTEEN SECONDS

THE GREAT CALIFORNIA EARTHQUAKE OF 1989

A book to benefit earthquake victims

THE TIDES FOUNDATION

ISLAND PRESS

This book is dedicated to all the victims, heroes and volunteers of the great California earthquake of 1989.

EDITORS' NOTE

Photojournalists are the eyes of the world. As such, they are often asked to record dire circumstances; sometimes at their own peril. They must remain detached from the horror they witness, but this professional necessity does not stop them from caring deeply. This book was born of the desire to give something back, to somehow help the people who suffered during this disaster.

The men and women who made the images in this book were working under extreme conditions. Through their eyes, with the passage of time, we are now able to see the pain, loss and ultimate strength of the people who endured this natural catastrophe.

Our heartfelt gratitude goes to the photographers, editors and scores of volunteers who contributed freely in order to bring some relief to the victims left behind after the photos were taken.

David Cohen   Doug Menuez   Ron Grant Tussy

"San Franciscans are used to earthquakes, but this one was different. The houses didn't squeak, the houses roared. The earth moved back and forth as if it was in a big box and somebody was shaking it back and forth. In the distance, from the north of the city, the smoke began to fill the skies. And the whole sky beyond the north part of the Bay was lit up and burning from the horrible fires that came out of the Marina District. Then we heard, very vaguely, that the Bay Bridge had collapsed. That was real scary.

"People in the neighborhoods then started getting together and turning to each other for support. Neighbors who'd never met each other started finding out who their neighbors were and began to do what neighbors are supposed to do, which is take care of each other.

"I think we all believe that we are the masters of the universe. We in our enlightened age have clean water, and we have heat, and we have all these things that we never question. And then something like this happens, and you realize that we are small creatures still."

— Randy Shilts, *The San Francisco Chronicle*

"A few days after the main shudder, they told us the quake had lasted only 15 seconds. But that is in real time. Earthquake time isn't real time.

"Or maybe the truth is, earthquake time is the most real time of all, a time when all the bull ceases and the preciousness of life is understood most acutely. In earthquake time, nobody gives a damn about a rebounding Dow or the Giants being down in the World Series, two games to none. In earthquake time, the bashed-in fender of a new car is invisible, a broken leg is but a twitch, and the richest people in the world are the men, women and children who have someone to hold onto until the shaking stops.

"The big one of Oct. 17 was not an event we can or should forget or try to 'get over.' It was a traumatic experience that started in the depths of the earth and wreaked damage all the way to the depths of the psyche. The 7.1 quake and its unscheduled but inevitable big encore are simply facts of life we must learn to live with — as vigorously, humorously and gracefully as our combined human resources can allow us to do."

— Stephanie Salter, *The San Francisco Examiner*

"We travel to space and we conquer disease. We do so many things that make us seem so smart. Nature has a way of reminding us of the overwhelming power and force that shaped the universe. We felt 15 seconds of that force the other day. We are all sobered, humbled and perhaps matured by what we saw.

"We will go on. There are hurricanes in other parts of the country, tornadoes and terrible weather that sometimes freezes a whole city. We say how fortunate we are to live in California. We come out on sunny days in November with our shirts and jackets open. We feel as if we're the smartest people in America because we chose such a great place to live. And every once in a while, Nature comes along and reminds us that whatever we may do, Nature has the upper hand, when all is said and done."

— Robert Maynard, *The Oakland Tribune*

ABOVE
Baseball forgotten, a frightened boy
huddles against a row of seats at
Candlestick Park.
– **Photo: John Storey,
The San Francisco Examiner**

LEFT
Stunned fans in the lower deck of
Candlestick Park reacted with fear,
laughter and confusion.
– **Photo: Paul Kitagaki, Jr.,
The San Jose Mercury News**

A proud Giants fan shows his unshaken
loyalty.
– **Photo: Gary Reyes,**
The Oakland Tribune

Oakland Athletics pitcher Storm Davis
hugs his baby daughter Erin
on the field.
– **Photo: Skip Shuman,**
The Sacramento Bee/SYGMA

Giants pitcher Steve Bedrosian points
to the Park's damaged upper deck as
his teammates look on.
– **Photo: Elizabeth Mangelsdorf,
The San Francisco Examiner**

Oakland A's manager Tony LaRussa
leads his wife and daughter through
the postquake confusion.
**– Photo: Lois Bernstein,
The Sacramento Bee/SYGMA**

"I've never seen anything that violent. The ground went up and down. I went in the street, the freeway shook, then a part just came down and the rest slid on top. I saw people trying to get out."
— RICHARD REYNOLDS, MANAGER OF AN AUTO SHOP TWO BLOCKS FROM THE I-880 FREEWAY

❖

"I said to myself, 'Lord, don't let this span collapse,' and just about that time the span collapsed."
— DAVE RIEMAN OF OAKLAND, MOTORIST ON THE I-880 CYPRESS STREET VIADUCT

Smoke rises from the mangled top span of I-880 in Oakland minutes after it collapsed, killing 42 people.
— Photo: Michael Macor, The Oakland Tribune

Paramedics, police and volunteers
struggle to remove a victim from the
upper level of I-880.
– **Photo: Michael Macor,**
The Oakland Tribune

Ken Nelson guides John Stafford to
safety, while his wife, Maedell Stafford,
awaits rescue from the lower deck.
– **Photo: Roy Williams,**
The Oakland Tribune

"There was tremendous response by the people [of the neighborhood]. People were carrying the wounded on their backs down ladders, sometimes 40 feet or more. These people never knew whether the freeway was going to collapse again."
– HUGO GONZALES,
OAKLAND POLICE OFFICER

LEFT
A neighborhood volunteer joins in the grisly work of extricating victims from the shattered stretch of I-880.
– Photo: Michael Macor,
The Oakland Tribune

23

Beams of falling concrete flattened
a victim's vehicle on I-880.
– **Photo: Chuck Nacke,
Picture Group**

Paramedics rushed to save lives
as survivors were pulled from the
collapsed freeway.
– **Photo: Meri Simon**

The Oakland City Police responded
immediately with 100 extra officers
who worked 12-hour shifts through
the night and the next day.
– **Photo: Martin Klimek,
The Marin Independent Journal**

"I remember bracing myself as hard as I could, and I saw water in front of us. We were at a 30- or 40- degree angle. I had a lot of lightning thoughts like, 'I've got to get home to my daughter.' I thought, 'There's the Bay. We're going into the Bay. I don't want to end up in the Bay.'"

– JANICE FREIBURGER, MOTORIST ON THE BAY BRIDGE

ABOVE
A 250-ton section of the Bay Bridge collapsed. The seven-mile Bridge is used by half a million commuters on a normal workday.
– **Photo: Doug Menuez**

RIGHT
Bruce Stephen and Janice Freiburger survived when a portion of the Bridge prevented their car from falling into San Francisco Bay.
– **Photo: Skip Shuman,
The Sacramento Bee/SYGMA**

PRECEDING PAGE
Shaken commuters survey the Bay
Bridge minutes after the earthquake.
– **Photo: Steve Ringman,
The San Francisco Chronicle**

ABOVE
A rescue worker despairs over the body
of Anamafi Kalausa Moala — the only
fatality of the Bay Bridge collapse.
– **Photo: David Ake,
United Press International**

RIGHT
A paramedic comforts a victim rescued
from the I-880 freeway in Oakland.
– **Photo: Damon Burris**

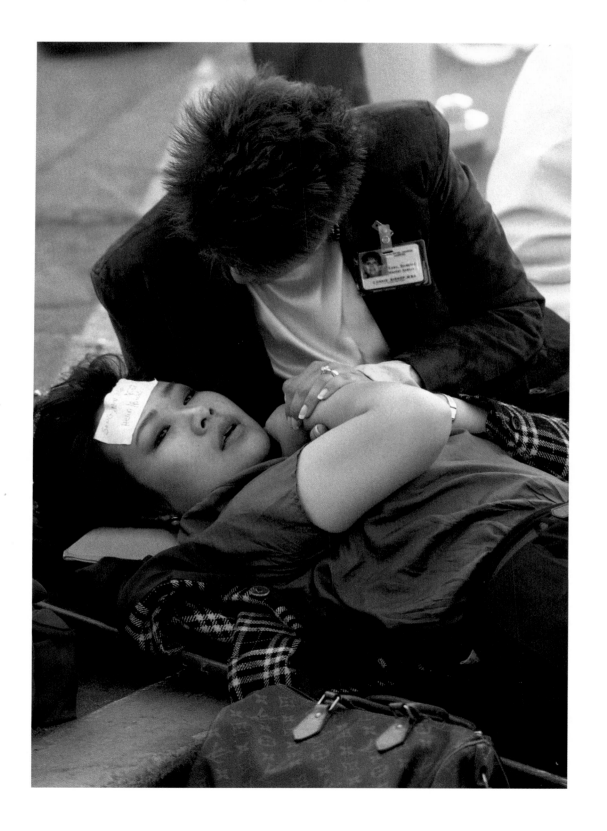

"I've been in Hurricane Hazel in Houston, I've been in fires, I've been in tornadoes, we've been robbed at gunpoint, but by God I've never felt anything like this."
— PHOEBE SEASE, SANTA CRUZ RESIDENT

LEFT
Citizens scramble to locate victims trapped in the rubble of Santa Cruz's Pacific Garden Mall.
— **Photo: Bill Lovejoy,
The Santa Cruz Sentinel**

BELOW
Edith Dominguez is rescued from under four feet of rubble at a department store in Santa Cruz.
— **Photo: Dan Coyro,
The Santa Cruz Sentinel**

"The definitive thing is, we don't know what the hell is going on here."
— MALCOLM CLARK OF THE U.S. GEOLOGICAL SURVEY IMMEDIATELY AFTER THE EARTHQUAKE

❖

"The radio kept telling everyone where to go to get food and water. I was crying, listening to it for the 50th time knowing I couldn't get there."
— BEVERLY SOLLARS, RESIDENT OF THE SANTA CRUZ MOUNTAINS, WHERE ROADS WERE MADE IMPASSABLE BY THE EARTHQUAKE

LEFT
Pacific Gas & Electric troubleshooter Bob Moyer leaps across a gaping fissure in the Santa Cruz mountains. PG&E crews worked feverishly around the clock to restore utility service to their customers.
– **Photo: Judy Griesedieck, The San Jose Mercury News**

TOP
Support pylons pierced the Harkins Slough Bridge, south of Watsonville, which buckled during the earthquake.
– **Photo: Richard Wisdom, The San Jose Mercury News**

BOTTOM
A gas explosion ignited and destroyed this house, located two blocks from the Pacific Garden Mall in Santa Cruz.
– **Photo: Dan Coyro, The Santa Cruz Sentinel**

Heather Zaknich of Santa Cruz
discovers her mother, Diana La
France, safe in the small mountain
community of Redwood Estates.
— **Photo: Michael Rondou,
The San Jose Mercury News**

The cross stands intact amid the
crumbled walls of St. Patrick's
Catholic Church, a Watsonville
landmark built of brick in 1903.
— **Photo: Warren Faidley**

"This is a natural disaster, an act of
God. When God speaks, everyone listens."

— REVEREND JESSE JACKSON

"I feel like I'm in a war zone," Jeanie yelled as we dashed around a police barricade and ran up the deserted street. On one corner a gas main had broken and was spewing gas and mud 10 feet into the air. A firefighter [shouted], "Go back! Go back! The whole block's gonna blow!"

– CONNIE BALLARD,
THE SAN FRANCISCO CHRONICLE

Aerial shots record the blaze in San Francisco's Marina District.
– **Photos: Martin Klimek,
The Marin Independent Journal**

ABOVE
Broken water mains forced Marina
resident Renato Canevari to collect
water from a leaking firehose coupling.
— **Photo: Timothy Baker,**
The Santa Rosa Press Democrat

RIGHT
Flash fires spread in the Marina from
the heat generated by a blaze that
destroyed a full city block. In an act
of desperation, a volunteer tosses
water on the flames.
— **Photo: Ross Pelton,**
The Marin Independent Journal

"I was talking to them ... a lady and a man, a couple. They had a lot of debris on them, so we had to cut another hole over where they were to try to remove some of the debris. But we didn't get to that point. The building started to go down, so we had to leave. Quite a few times I've gone over in my mind what else I could have done, maybe to get the lady out, who didn't make it .... It bothers you a little ... quite a bit, actually."

– TOM BAILON, FIREFIGHTER

RIGHT
Firefighters combat the five-alarm fire that blazed for over five hours in the Marina District.
– Photo: Ron Grant Tussy

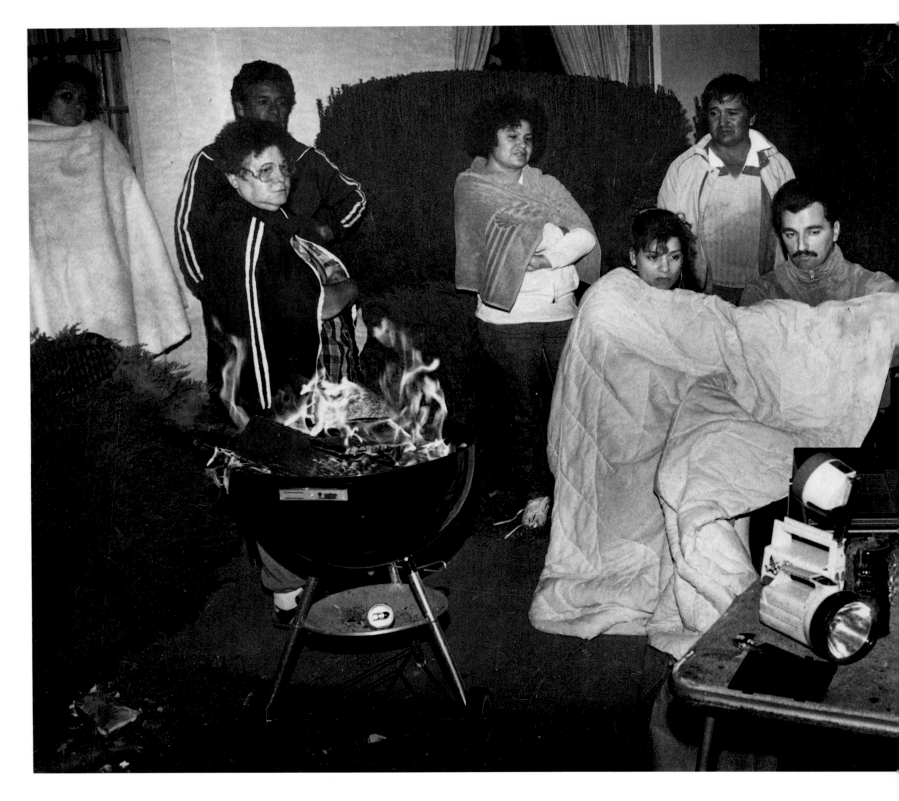

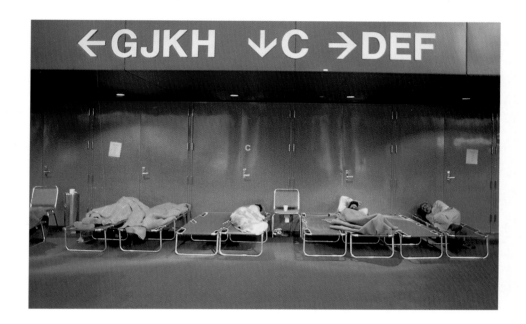

"I don't know why I'm buying these groceries. I don't have anywhere to go."
— WEEPING MAN AT A MARKET IN SANTA CRUZ

❖

"People lost a part of their identity. They lost part of their history …. It's more than a piece of property. It's a symbol of life."
— CRAIG WOLFE, COUNSELOR AT THE LOS GATOS FEDERAL EMERGENCY MANAGEMENT AGENCY

LEFT
Afraid to enter their home, the Ceballos family of Watsonville camp in their yard.
– Photo: Steve Castillo, The San Francisco Chronicle

ABOVE
Hundreds of San Franciscans made homeless by the quake found shelter at the Moscone Convention Center.
– Photo: Timothy Baker, The Santa Rosa Press Democrat

"How fragile our lives are – you take so much for granted…. You have to see [the devastation] to know how fortunate we all are that we survived. You learn to count your blessings."

—STEVE PARLICK, BYSTANDER IN THE MARINA

PRECEDING PAGE
Like thousands of other Northern Californians who jammed phone lines seeking news of friends and loved ones, Marina resident Jim Eimers makes contact with his roommate. Neighbor Jack Haskel, 5, listens in.
– **Photo: Katy Raddatz, The San Francisco Examiner**

ABOVE
Makeshift camps in Alamo Square shelter San Francisco residents.
– **Photo: Blake Sell, Reuters**

LEFT
Mary Francis Johnson and her son Jordan sleep in a park across from an emergency center in San Francisco.
– **Photo: Kim Komenich, The San Francisco Examiner**

"There was and is a certain wildness in the air, a 'tomorrow we die' attitude based on the unspoken awareness that the Earth could open up in the next instant and swallow it all – from the baroque palaces of Nob Hill to the gaming houses of the Barbary Coast.

"We realize afresh the joys and dangers of living here, and we reaffirm our belief that it is worth the gamble, however great."
– HERB CAEN, THE SAN FRANCISCO CHRONICLE

LEFT
A newly homeless Marina resident sets up camp in the shadow of the Palace of Fine Arts, the last remaining building from the Panama-Pacific Exhibition of 1915.
– **Photo: Vince Maggiora, The San Francisco Chronicle**

A San Francisco fireman searches for victims in the rubble of the Marina District fire, which claimed three lives.
– Photo: Paul Kitagaki, Jr., The San Jose Mercury News

An abandoned cat is the sole inhabitant of this condemned house in the Marina District.
– Photo: Elizabeth Mangelsdorf, The San Francisco Examiner

"I was feeling sorry for myself because I couldn't find something that fell off my shelf. Then a seven-year-old boy came by and said he couldn't find his house."

— CYNDI FORBES, SANTA CRUZ RESIDENT

Ten-year-old Apollo Terry peers at the ashes of a neighbor's home in downtown Santa Cruz.
– **Photo: Jason Grow, The San Jose Mercury News**

"I just had to come down here today to take a long look at what remains of my life."
— DAVID THOLKOWSKY, A SAN FRANCISCO
MARINA RESIDENT WHOSE HOME COLLAPSED

LEFT
Kellie Oblinger clutches her Elvis clock, one of the undamaged items remaining in the Santa Cruz home she shares with Rhonda Botello.
– Photo: Karen Borchers,
The San Jose Mercury News

59

"It was my worst nightmare come true. I'm just glad to be alive. As I lay under the rubble, I could hear the people calling out, but they couldn't hear me until I began to bang on a door with a pipe."
— SHERRA COX, RESCUED FROM HER MARINA DISTRICT HOME

RIGHT
Firefighters scale ladders to search for more victims of the Marina fire.
— Photo: Paul Kitagaki, Jr.,
The San Jose Mercury News

60

"That was a three-story building. It just went down like an accordion."
— SGT. ROGER BATTAGLIA, SAN FRANCISCO POLICE DEPARTMENT

OPPOSITE PAGE TOP
The top floor of a two-story apartment building spills into the street in San Francisco's Marina District.
– **Photo: Timothy Baker,**
The Santa Rosa Press Democrat

OPPOSITE PAGE BOTTOM
The owner of the crushed car had just entered this four-story building when the earthquake struck. She escaped by crawling through a top-floor window onto the street.
– **Photo: Lloyd Francis, Jr.,**
The Fresno Bee

LEFT
All but a few of the buildings in San Francisco's financial district withstood the force of the earthquake.
– **Photo: Skip Shuman,**
The Sacramento Bee/SYGMA

A young boy explores a quake-scarred
Marina District street.
– **Photo: James Aronovsky,
Picture Group**

Mark Liljagren of Palo Alto
surveys an enormous fissure near
the earthquake's epicenter in
Santa Cruz County.
– **Photo: Jeff Reinking,
Picture Group**

Sludge oozed onto San Francisco's
Marina Green as a result of quake-
caused liquefaction, a phenomenon
which transformed the landfill below
ground into a fluid mass.
– **Photo: Timothy Baker,
The Santa Rosa Press Democrat**

The awesome destruction drew
hundreds of spectators to the edge
of police lines in the Marina District.
– **Photo: George Nikitin**

"It was more like *The Exorcist* than an earthquake. It threw us all over and into each other. I was watching my friend Phoebe fly by me, smashing from one wall into the other. I was trying to grab her, but couldn't get her. I finally got her on the third try before she flew out the window."

— JOE FORST, SANTA CRUZ RESIDENT

LEFT
Hollister resident Dorothy Blackie salvages drapes from her lifelong home that slid off its foundation.
– **Photo: Michael Williamson, The Sacramento Bee/SYGMA**

"There is no greater betrayal than when the earth defaults on the understanding that it stay under foot while we go about the business of life, which is full enough of perils as it is."
— JERRY CARROLL, THE SAN FRANCISCO CHRONICLE

LEFT
Lucy Reed waits to be evacuated from her home, which sits in the shadow of the crumbled Cypress Street viaduct.
— Photo: Reginald Pearman,
The Oakland Tribune

Pearl Sears Lake stands outside the damaged Santa Cruz home her parents had moved into the night of the 1906 earthquake.
– **Photo: Shmuel Thaler**

RIGHT

A Watsonville family is still sheltered by tent in Ramsay Park 10 days after the quake.
– **Photo: Michael Williamson, The Sacramento Bee/SYGMA**

FOLLOWING PAGES:
TOP LEFT
Ramsay Park in Watsonville is transformed into a tent city for 150 urban refugees.

BOTTOM LEFT
Homeless earthquake victims line up outside the Ramsay Park Camp in Watsonville to collect donations from toy companies.

TOP RIGHT
Near Watsonville Airport, quake victims sort through a pile of clothes sent by donors from around the state.

BOTTOM RIGHT
José Valasquez, 8, and his father await an uncertain future in Watsonville.
– **Photos: Michael Williamson, The Sacramento Bee/SYGMA**

"We've had our myth of invulnerability punctured. Something like this forces people to stop the denial, to stop thinking that they are immortal."
— DANIEL WEISS, PSYCHOLOGIST,
UNIVERSITY OF CALIFORNIA, SAN FRANCISCO

A woman and her child pray for Walter Butler, their minister at the Taylor Chapel in Vallejo. Butler was killed in the I-880 collapse.
– **Photo: H. Darr Beiser, USA Today**

Religious treasures top a pile of salvaged belongings in Watsonville's Callahan Park.
– **Photo: Tom Van Dyke,
The San Jose Mercury News**

"Gradually, it began to sink in: Today, there are people dead, people homeless… the fires are not fireworks, and this is not a movie."
— HERBERT GOLD, THE LOS ANGELES TIMES

RIGHT
San Francisco Mayor Art Agnos, center, confers with California's Lt. Governor Leo McCarthy outside the city's emergency command center on Turk Street.
– **Photo: Kim Komenich, The San Francisco Examiner**

President George Bush reviews quake
damage estimates with Speaker of
the California Assembly Willie Brown,
San Francisco Mayor Art Agnos,
Congresswoman Nancy Pelosi and
Oakland Mayor Lionel Wilson.
– **Photo: Larry Downing, Newsweek**

President Bush meets with Santa
Cruz Mayor Mardi Wormhoudt
and Congressman Leon Panetta.
– **Photo: Bill Lovejoy,
The Santa Cruz Sentinel**

"Inherent in the national coverage was a sensationalistic approach. By putting the news anchors in front of that same collapsed apartment building in the Marina, one would think it was typical of the whole city. It was a pathetic ratings grab which worried people needlessly."
– JOHN DVORAK,
THE SAN FRANCISCO EXAMINER

OPPOSITE PAGE
NBC News Anchor Tom Brokaw prepares for a broadcast.
– Photo: Paul Kitagaki, Jr.,
The San Jose Mercury News

TOP
From atop a mobile camera unit close to the Cypress Street viaduct, CBS' Dan Rather anchors the news the evening after the earthquake.
– Photo: John Trotter,
The Sacramento Bee/SYGMA

BOTTOM
Today Show anchor Bryant Gumbel interviews San Francisco Mayor Art Agnos near Bay and Fillmore streets.
– Photo: Jason Grow,
The San Jose Mercury News

ABOVE

Lorrie Helm, ex-wife of Buck Helm, talks to the press with her son Jeff and daughter Desiree at Highland Hospital. Buck was rescued after being trapped for four days in a collapsed section of I-880. He died of complications on November 18th.
– **Photo: John Roca,**
New York Daily News

RIGHT

Daniel Rubi waits on the second day of his vigil for his son, Juan, who was trapped under the Cypress Street viaduct. Juan's body was eventually found.
– **Photo: Mark Aronoff,**
The Santa Rosa Press Democrat

PRECEDING PAGE
Residents of the Marina District
push carts they'll use to collect
belongings from their damaged
homes and apartments.
– **Photo: Jeff Reinking,**
Picture Group

ABOVE
Donna Casa of Morgan Hill, who lost
her home, was among the minority of
Bay Area residents to have full
earthquake coverage. Her insurance
agent, Bob Steese, presents her with a
$20,000 check for living expenses.
– **Photo: Judy Griesedieck,**
The San Jose Mercury News

California Conservation Corps
members rescue possessions from
toppled houses on Divisadero Street
in San Francisco's Marina District.
**– Photo: Fred Larson,
The San Francisco Chronicle**

"You guys have five minutes more," came the call from the street as a bed mattress came sailing through the air and hit the wet pavement with a smack. "Three minutes," came another call. "You guys have to wind it up in there. You guys have to get out of there – your time is up," came the final call.

— CITY INSPECTORS MONITORING MARINA RESIDENTS DURING THE FIFTEEN MINUTES THEY WERE GIVEN TO COLLECT THEIR POSSESSIONS

"It's a very tough thing to condemn a home, to demolish a home. We've had to do both. For the most part the people have been very, very cooperative. I hope they know [we have] their best interest in mind."

– DON McCONLOGUE, ASSISTANT SUPERINTENDENT, SAN FRANCISCO DEPARTMENT OF PUBLIC WORKS

LEFT
Two days after the quake, an emergency crew from the California Conservation Corps forms a human chain to remove bricks trapping Robin Ortiz at the Santa Cruz Coffee Roasting Co. The effort did not prove successful. Ortiz did not survive.
– **Photo: Shmuel Thaler**

ABOVE
A displaced resident shaves in a Red Cross relief center at the Marina Middle School.
– **Photo: Chuck Nacke, Picture Group**

"The tunnel was moving, the bridge was moving, all the cars were sliding around like they were on ice. The suspension cables were swinging back and forth, like a giant harp somebody was playing. Then everybody started slowly driving off the Bridge, at about 25 miles an hour. It wasn't fast enough for me. All I wanted was to get off that bridge."

— BAY BRIDGE MOTORIST BUCK HALL OF SAN FRANCISCO

LEFT
A television cameraman surveys the deserted Bay Bridge three days after the quake.
— Photo: Kent Porter, The Santa Rosa Press Democrat

LEFT
The irreparably damaged section of
the Bay Bridge is lowered onto a barge.
– **Photo: Paul Richards,
United Press International**

RIGHT
California Dept. of Transportation
(Caltrans) crews work to remove
the damaged lower section of the
Bay Bridge a week after the quake.
– **Photo: Eric Lars Risberg,
Associated Press**

An anonymous donor left this
memorial to those killed in the
Cypress Street viaduct collapse.
– **Photo: Gary Sinick**

This unstable portion of the heavily
traveled Embarcadero Freeway
in San Francisco is closed to traffic.
– **Photo: Craig Lee,
The San Francisco Examiner**

On the first Monday after the quake,
a ferry heads for San Francisco near the
damaged and desolate Bay Bridge.
– **Photo: Tom Duncan,
The Oakland Tribune**

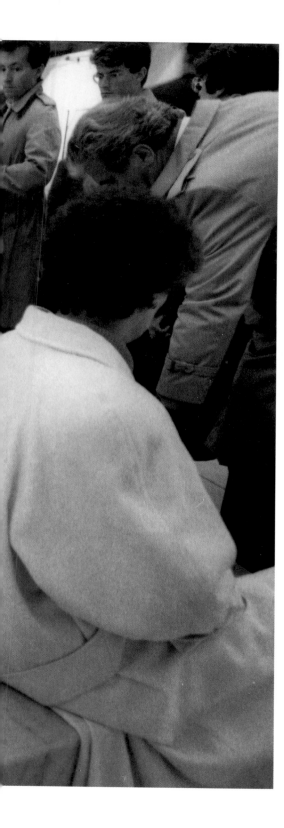

LEFT
A man naps in a crowded BART station. After the earthquake, the number of BART commuters jumped over 50% to an average of 325,000 passengers per day.
– **Photo: Katy Raddatz,
The San Francisco Examiner**

ABOVE
Exhausted BART commuters travel under the Bay.
– **Photo: John Trotter,
The Sacramento Bee/SYGMA**

"This is the only time I've ever been scared in this ballpark."
— WILLIE MAYS, FORMER SAN
FRANCISCO GIANTS OUTFIELDER

A structural engineer checks for damage to Candlestick Park's canopy the day after the earthquake.
— **Photo: Michael Williamson,
The Sacramento Bee/SYGMA**

San Francisco 49er fans, displaced by the temporary closure of Candlestick Park, yell for their team at Stanford Stadium four days after the earthquake. The sign is from the people of hard-hit Hollister.
– **Photo: Rick Perry,**
The Sacramento Bee/SYGMA

Twelve heroes threw the opening pitch to resume the World Series at Candlestick Park 10 days after the earthquake.
– **Photo: Paul Kitagaki, Jr.,**
The San Jose Mercury News

Residents of San Francisco's Marina District watch the demolition of a neighbor's house.
— **Photo: Elizabeth Mangelsdorf, The San Francisco Examiner**

October 17, a day which will long be remembered for the destruction it brought to Northern California, brought joy to Marilyn Cupples of Santa Cruz, who holds baby Elizabeth, born at 5:03pm, a minute before the quake hit.
— **Photo: Shmuel Thaler**

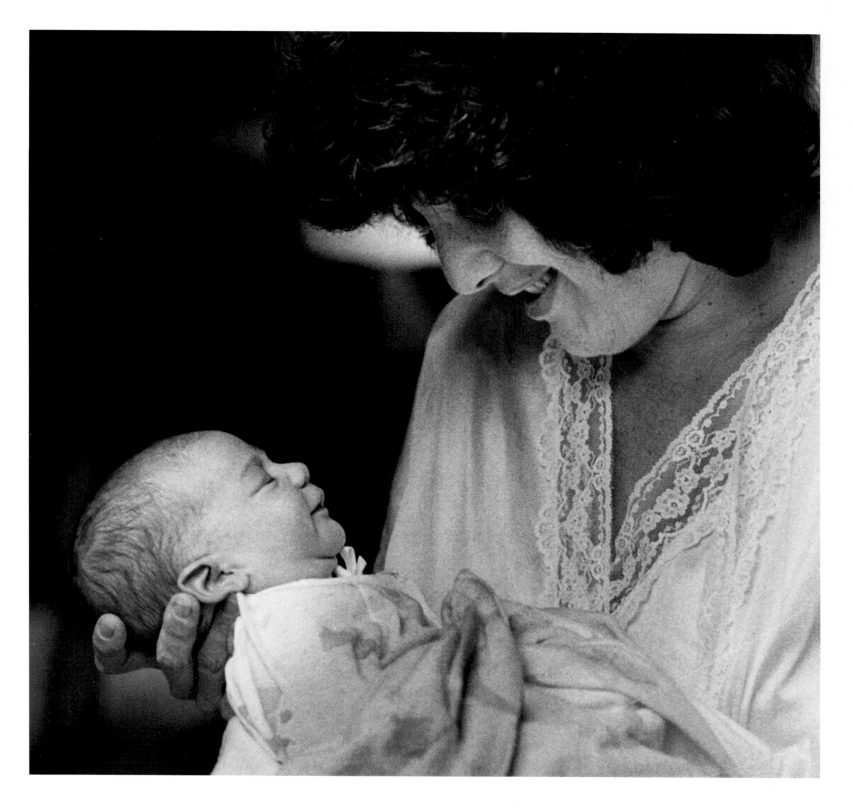

"Months or years from now when the minutiæ and disappointments
have clouded our vision, when we once again find ourselves doubting the
basic goodness that lies in the human soul, the instinctive courage that
simmers unseen in the common man and woman, we must remember
that fallen highway and the human ladder pressed against it."
— STEPHANIE SALTER, THE SAN FRANCISCO EXAMINER

RIGHT
Billie Jean Mosher comforts her half-
sister Alexandria Harris during a
memorial service for quake victims at
Glide Memorial Methodist Church
in San Francisco.
— **Photo: Frankie Frost,**
The Marin Independent Journal

October 17, 1989, was a rare day in San Francisco from the moment it began – a balmy, made-to-order, Indian summer day that made you feel glad to be alive. At 5:00pm, anticipation hung in the air as sports fans of the world tuned into the Bay Area for game three of the Oakland-San Francisco World Series. And at 5:04, the earth shook — violently and relentlessly for 15 seconds.

Some of the nation's finest photojournalists, including those here to capture the excitement of the World Series, were catapulted into action. They were to record the greatest earthquake to hit Northern California since 1906. Shutters clicked, capturing the fear in the faces of the fans and players at Candlestick Park. As the evening progressed, news spread of the immediate death and destruction on Interstate 880 in Oakland and of the staggering collapse of a portion of the Bay Bridge.

Reports trickled in that Santa Cruz, near the epicenter, took the earthquake's hardest blows. When darkness fell, the rising plume of smoke above blacked-out San Francisco sent an unmistakable signal that the disaster was far from over.

Often at great risk to themselves, photographers instinctively recorded the casualties and documented the horror, despair, heroism and hope of the day. They were witnessing a natural disaster, the full toll of which would not be known for weeks. Before their job was over, they would all be touched by the grief and human suffering they were capturing on film.

Freelance photographer Ron Tussy saw the raging fire in San Francisco's Marina District through binoculars from his hilltop home across the Bay in Sausalito. He threw his camera bags in his car and raced across the Golden Gate Bridge to San Francisco's Marina District.

"The further I went into the area, the more grotesque the buildings looked," Tussy said. "Firemen were desperately trying to hook up hoses to the fire hydrants, and nothing but mud was coming out. I heard a fireman say, 'We might lose this whole part of the city,' and visions of the 1906 fire and earthquake swept over me."

On assignment for *Newsweek*, Tussy spent the next four days covering the rescue at I-880, the ravaged Marina and the devastation in Santa Cruz. He returned home exhausted and drained. Unable to shake images of the quake, an idea came to Ron that wouldn't let go. "I decided I had to try to do something to help. I wanted to get other photographers nationwide to donate their pictures to make a book to benefit earthquake victims."

Tussy called fellow photojournalist Doug Menuez. The book idea wouldn't let go of Menuez either. "I called David Cohen, who I knew could tell me whether the book could be done," Menuez remembered. Director of the *Day in the Life* photo book series, Cohen said, "Great idea, but it has to be done in 7 to 10 days."

"I thought it would be impossible, but we had to try," Menuez recalled.

Menuez' next call was to Susan Wels and Maureen Healy of Healy/Wels Communications. "I knew we'd need really good word and idea people to get this thing rolling. I was glad they thought it was a great idea and wanted to get involved."

The first meeting was held six days after the earthquake. Tussy, Menuez, Cohen, Wels and Healy discussed contacts and logistics. Cohen laid out the bottom line. "This is a book that would normally take a year and a half to put together," he said. "We were going to do it in a couple of weeks."

To pull it off, Cohen, Tussy and Menuez recruited a core team of talented, committed volunteers. By night the small circle of organizers had grown to include attorney Philip Feldman of Coblentz, Cahen, McCabe & Breyer; Stephanie Sherman, production director at Collins Publishers; Tom Ridge of Omnicomp-Omnicolor; and Carole Bidnick, sales director for Collins Publishers.

"We were sitting in a circle in David's living room, when suddenly another tremor rocked our chairs," Bidnick remembered. "For a split second there was silence, followed by black humor about the book being obsolete before it was even completed."

Then it was back to business. And the group resumed the conversation as if earthquakes weren't part of our future – just bad memories to be documented for the relief of victims and for history.

As we sat in that circle, brainstorming ideas on how to get the necessary equipment, talent and funds to make the book a reality, Cohen slipped away to make a phone call to the general manager of Eastman Kodak's Professional Photography Department, Raymond DeMoulin. He came back with a financial commitment from Kodak that would provide the initial funding. The book was really going to happen.

The next day telephones rang and arrangements were made with the speed of a fast-moving train. Healy drafted a project fact sheet, convinced West Coast Properties to donate office space for headquarters on Battery Street in San Francisco and sent out requests for volunteers. Tussy called Fireman's Fund Insurance Company and the project had another major financial contributor. Menuez called Apple Computer for help. Jane Anderson of Apple's public relations firm and Keri Walker in Apple's internal public relations department simply asked, "What do you want and when?"

The next morning, we had a bank of Apple computers in our new offices. Feldman began talks with The Tides Foundation, which would sponsor the project, oversee the distribution of funds raised, and serve as publisher with its affiliate, Island Press. Bidnick got agreements from Harper & Row and Publishers Group West to distribute the book for free, and early orders for the book-in-progress started coming in.

On Thursday, Susan Hailey joined the operation and recruited and directed dozens of volunteers. A Harvard MBA, Hailey was the ideal person to create and manage the office systems.

On the photography front, things were quickly falling into place. "We nailed down each source as best we could until all the newspapers, national magazines and wire services were participating. Considering that these were competing publications, it was phenomenal that we got their film, editors and cooperation," said Menuez.

All the major Bay Area newspapers jumped on board, contributing film and, in some cases, photo editors. "The news magazines were no problem," Tussy added. "But we were on pins and needles trying to get film from AP and UPI. We expected the agencies like GAMMA, SYGMA and SIPA to be even tougher – pictures are their livelihood and they can't afford to give up a single frame for free. But they immediately did."

When the nuts and bolts part of the project began, we all felt fortunate that we were so close to Silicon Valley and top technological talent. "Where else in the world could you parachute into an empty office with a bank of Apple computers and printers, Farallon networking, Adobe software, Nikon and Barneyscan scanners, Mass Micro storage disks and drives, SuperMac monitors and National Instruments boards to produce a book within two weeks?" asked Menuez.

Research engineers Chris Thorman and Barry Haynes of Apple Computer joined the staff and immediately began providing technical support. "Everyone agreed we were pushing the envelope of desktop publishing in putting this book together," remembered Cohen. "The mere fact that all these companies made this cutting-edge technology available for free and set it up in a matter of hours qualifies as a miracle."

A talented team from *MacWEEK*, including Elinor Craig, Jonathan Hornstein, Connie Guglielmo, Janice Maloney and Dan Farber, quickly set up the database for logging and tracking photo captions and quotes, editing late into the night.

As more than 10,000 images came in the door, the photo editors sprang into action, cataloging them with the help of Charlotte Gay. The arduous editing process began as George Wedding of *The Sacramento Bee* was joined on the photo editing team by Beth Renneisen of *The Marin Independent Journal*, Sandra Eisert of *The San Jose Mercury News*, Dave Wyland of *Newsweek* and Penni Gladstone of *The San Francisco Examiner*. Along with Cohen, Tussy and Menuez, they sifted through approximately ten thousand photos to find the images that would tell the whole story of the 1989 earthquake in 120 pages.

When it came time for the second round of editing, Healy/Wels Communications issued an open invitation to the press to come see first-hand the incredible production effort. As news cameras zoomed-in over their shoulders, the photo editors and core group members engaged in passionate debate over the fate of each of the 200 photographs to survive the second edit.

In the final exhaustive editing session, the core group and others shouted their votes as 150 selects were pared down to fill a mere 90 slots available in the book. Soon black-and-white scans of the edited photos littered the production room walls, and the designers began to make sense of it all.

Through it all, Cohen helped Tussy and Menuez guide the editorial and design process. "After nine years of producing photographic books at a high-speed pace, I thought this would be a great opportunity to use my skills to give something back," said Cohen.

As work progressed, word of the project was getting out around the country. At a press conference on Wednesday, November 1, newspaper, radio and television reporters gathered to hear Tussy, Menuez, Cohen and Wedding share their stories of putting the historic book together.

With the cameras gone, the design team worked under the direction of graphic designer Cecil Juanarena to perfect the photo spreads that take readers from the chaos and horror experienced by quake victims to the progressive rebuilding of a Bay Area that never lost hope or its spirit of community.

On Friday, it was time for Cohen and Menuez to return to real life. Tussy stayed on to supervise the final phase of work. Sherman took over at the production helm of *15 Seconds*, and Healy and Wels saw the book through final text editing with help from Craig. What many said could not be done was done in just 10 days.

The book would be off Cal Central's press before Thanksgiving. And we all had many thanks to give. We had survived the quake and the making of the book about the quake.

As proceeds from book sales brought much needed long-term relief to earthquake victims, we would know that our efforts helped make a difference in the lives of those who were not so fortunate. In years to come, all of us would be able to look at *15 Seconds* and relive the events that changed our lives.

Of the many photojournalists involved, perhaps Timothy Baker of *The Santa Rosa Press Democrat* said it best. "As photojournalists, you think you're doing a service when you photograph a tragedy. But *15 Seconds* was a way to make up for all the times I wanted to put my cameras down and lend a hand. It was a healing process for all of us."

– By Maureen Healy and Susan Wels

CREDITS

Project Directors
David Cohen
Doug Menuez
Ron Grant Tussy

Photo Editors
David Cohen
Sandra Eisert, *The San Jose Mercury News*
Penni Gladstone, *The San Francisco Examiner*
Doug Menuez, photographer
Beth Renneisen, *The Marin Independent Journal*
Ron Grant Tussy, photographer
George Wedding, *The Sacramento Bee*
Dave Wyland, *Newsweek*

Text Editors
Maureen Healy
Susan Wels

Editorial Contributors
Elinor Craig
Dan Farber
Connie Guglielmo
Jonathan Hornstein
Janice Maloney

General Manager
Susan Hailey

Art Director
Cecil Juanarena

Director of Production
Stephanie Sherman

Systems Design Integration
Tom Ridge

Production Coordinator
Kathryn Yuschenkoff

Promotion
Healy/Wels Communications

Sales Director
Carole Bidnick

Raster Image Processing
Omnicomp/Omnicolor

Printing
Cal Central Press

Technical Consultants
Barry Haynes
Chris Thorman

Attorneys
William K. Coblentz
Philip B. Feldman
Coblentz, Cahen, McCabe & Breyer

MAJOR SPONSORS

Eastman Kodak Company
Fireman's Fund Insurance Company
Apple Computer, Inc.
Oppenheimer Management Corporation

IN-KIND SPONSORS

Adobe Systems, Inc.
Aero Delivery
Audio Video Services of San Francisco
Barneyscan
BMUG
Blue Print Service Group
Burrelle's Press Clipping Service
Bus Van
Cal Central Press
Collins Publishers, Inc.
DayStar
DEST, Inc.
Farallon Computing, Inc.
General Graphics
Graphic Coating, Inc.
Harper & Row Publishers
Howard, Rice, Nemerouski, Canady,
    Robertson, and Falk
Il Fornaio Gastronomia
Imagine That Design Studio
Jeff Munroe Photography
Kirk Paper Company
Krishna Copy Center
A. L. Lemos Company
Letraset
Lucas Trucking
MacOrchard
MacWEEK
Mass Microsystems
Midtown Stationers
National Instruments

Nikon, Inc.
Omnicomp-Omnicolor
Peripheral Land Inc.
Pinnacle Sales International
Printmasters Embarcadero
Professional Color Laboratory
Publishers Group West
Rudy Gomez Photo/Arts
Safeway
Samy's Camera
Speedway DTP/Sansome
Studio Reflex Design
SuperMac Technology
The Exploratorium
The New Lab
West Coast Properties
Zellerbach Paper Company

CONTRIBUTORS

Jane Anderson
Edvin Bang-Knudsen
Dennis Biggs
Lezlie R. Bishop
James Brown
Russell Brown
Guy Cooper
Kasey Cotulla
George Craig
Jim Clark
Raymond DeMoulin
Bob Ditter

Robert Eichemeyer
Randy Fleming
Kevin Greene
Ernie Haskins
Les Howell
Jan Johns
Scott Keilholtz
Judy Land
Rick Lemos
Theodore Lucia
William Maher
Thomas McFadden
Vicki Olds
Drummond Pike
Bob Pugh
Brian O'Reilly
Jeanie Rader
Gordon Saul
Marc Seager
Nancy Sobin-Dreyer
Ron Taniwaki
Gary Todoroff
Jim Toland
Bob Truelove
Keri Walker
Judy Wheeler
Bill Wignall
Paul Wiley
Charlie Winton
Mike Winton
Pete Zogas

MANY THANKS TO:

Lexine Alpert	Brian Hajducek	Craig Mitchell
Carmen Arbona	Steven Hailey	Richard Moore
Timothy Baker	Chris Hallihan	Amy Neiman
Cathy Baldwin	Tom Hedges	Fran Ortiz
Robin Barker	Sibylla Herbrich	Diana Parks
Jenny Barry	Linda Hoppe	Nancy Pelosi
Keith Baumann	William Hutton	Rod Perkins
Ron Bingham	Alex Ivanov	Jeanie Rader
Jeff Braverman	Leslie Jonath	Tom Reilly
Louis J. Brazil	Steven Johnides	Patti Richards
Bernard Burk	Joan Kampe	Nayla Rizk
Bill Carey	Susan Keefe	Monte Rosen
Amy Christen	Alex Keenan	Cary Sadler
Simon Clephan	Suzie Keith	Rick Schaut
Jenny Collins	Wendy Keogh	Kathy Seligman
Allen Crider	Jackie Kileen	Eric Slomanson
Harry Crutchfield	Edgar Kitchen	Peter Smith
Mary Defenderfer	Elizabeth Latasa	Polly Smith
Susan DeVinny	Regis Lefebure	Ann Krueger Spivack
Ken Doyle	Mary Margaret Lewis	John Steele
Laura Ducoff	Mike Liebhold	Rose Steele
Ted Evans	Debra Lynn	John Clay Stites
Dan Farber	Maria Tereza Machado	Delly Tamer
Lisa Brent Feldman	Marcia Makino	Jon Tandler
Hope Feldman	Janice Maldneg	Janet Thomas
Paul Finkle	Janice Maloney	Simon Trapp
Henri Froissart	James W. McCall	Sheba Veghte
Charlotte Gay	Lauren McGuire	Karen Warner
Morris Glickstein	Pam McQuesten	Clair Whitmer
Bruce Gray	Margo Meier-Bachtol	Bill Woodcock
Kathy Haas	Paolo Xaviar Machado Menuez	Mark Zimmer

This book was produced in record time on Apple Macintosh computers using the latest in desktop publishing technology.

Farallon Computing donated its PhoneNET hardware and Timbuktu networking software, which was used extensively to send files back and forth among the nine Macintoshes. A team from BMUG helped to install and maintain the network.

After the photo editing process, the more than 200 images were scanned into the Macintoshes by a volunteer team working day and night, so the design team of Cecil Juanarena and Stephanie Sherman could begin working on the layouts.

Ron Taniwaki and Mike Phillips of Nikon provided us with the critical color image scanners to help us meet our deadlines. In addition, Barneyscan, Apple and Howtek color and black-and- white image scanners were used to digitize the images.

Various software packages were used to scan low resolution versions of the photographs into an unusually powerful Macintosh IIX computer. It contained a 40MHz CPU accelerator from DayStar and 32 megabytes of RAM memory on the motherboard from Pinnacle Sales International. The low resolution images were used in page design. Two pre-release image editing software packages were used to generate high resolution images which appear on pages 62 and 63. ColorStudio, from Letraset, was used to scan the photos, and Photoshop, from Adobe Systems, Inc., was used to generate the color separations and duotones on those pages. In addition, Aldus' FreeHand 2.02 was used to create and separate the locator map that appears on the right. Traditional color separation techniques were used for the remaining images in the book.

In addition to an electronic network, a "SneakerNet" was set up to transport the massive image data files and layouts stored on Mass Microsystems' 45MB removable cartridges.

Stephanie Sherman of Collins Publishing and Tom Ridge of Omnicomp-Omnicolor supervised the production process and integration of the electronic separations with separations created by traditonal means.

Text was created using Microsoft Word 4.0 and Microsoft Works. Tracking photos and quotes was done in Claris Corp.'s FileMaker II. The photo layouts, including the text and graphics, were laid out using Aldus' PageMaker 3.02.

Finally the layouts for position and size were output on Omnicomp's Linotronic raster image processor. The high-resolution text films, also generated by the Linotronic, followed in a matter of days.

PRINTER – Cal Central Press, Sacramento, CA. Cover: Miller 6-color sheetfed offset press. Text: Harris M300 6-color heatset web offset press.

TYPOGRAPHY – Adobe Systems, Inc.; Adobe Garamond & Adobe Garamond Expert Set – Emigre Graphics; Matrix and Modula Bold.

PAPER – Cover: Kirk Paper 12pt. Brilliant Art Gloss C1S. Text: Zellerbach Sonoma Gloss Book 100#.

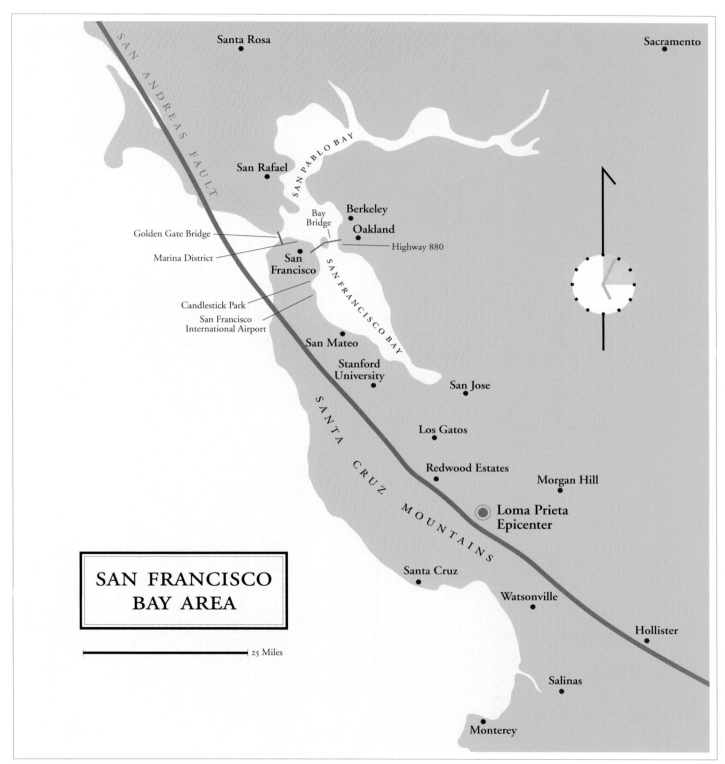

Santa Rosa

Sacramento

SAN ANDREAS FAULT

SAN PABLO BAY

San Rafael

Bay
Bridge

Berkeley

Oakland

Golden Gate Bridge

Highway 880

Marina District

San
Francisco

SAN FRANCISCO BAY

Candlestick Park

San Francisco
International Airport

San Mateo

Stanford
University

San Jose

Los Gatos

Redwood Estates

Morgan Hill

SANTA CRUZ MOUNTAINS

◉ Loma Prieta
Epicenter

Santa Cruz

Watsonville

Hollister

SAN FRANCISCO
BAY AREA

25 Miles

Salinas

Monterey

MAP: Chris Thorman